Goodnight Lullabies

Illustrated by Jeff Shelly

Disney PRESS

NEW YORK

1 3 5 7 9 10 8 6 4 2

Library of Congress Catalog Card Number: 91-71345
ISBN: 1-56282-054-0

Contents

The Dustman

When the toys are growing weary,
And the twilight gathers in;
When the nursery still echoes
With the children's merry din;

Then unseen, unheard, unnoticed
Comes an old man up the stair,
Lightly to the children passes,
Lays his hand upon their hair.

Softly smiles the good old Dustman;
In their eyes the dust he throws,
Till their little heads are falling,
And their weary eyes must close.

Then the Dustman very gently
Takes each little dimpled hand
Leads them through the sweet green
   shadows,
Far away in slumberland.

4

Sleep, Baby, Sleep

Sleep, baby, sleep,
Thy father tends the sheep,
Thy mother rocks the slumber-tree
And softly falls a dream for thee,
Sleep, baby, sleep.

Lullaby, My Pretty One

Lullaby, my pretty one,
Gone the day and set the sun.
Lullaby my pretty one,
And sleep until the morning,
And sleep until the morning.

7

Sleep, Sleep, Beauty Bright

Sleep, sleep, beauty bright,
Dreaming in the joys of night;
Sleep, sleep; in thy sleep
Little sorrows sit and weep.

Sweet babe, in thy face
Soft desires I can trace,
Secret joys and secret smiles,
Little pretty infant wiles.

As thy softest limbs I feel,
Smiles as of the morning steal
O'er thy cheek, and o'er thy breast
Where thy little heart doth rest.

Oh the cunning wiles that creep
In thy little heart asleep!
When thy little heart doth wake
Then the dreadful night shall break.

9

Sleep My Baby

Sleep my baby,
Sleep my darling,
Baby lullaby.
On your cradle
Moon is shining,
Softly from the sky.

I shall sing
And tell you stories,
If you close your eyes.
Slumber sweetly
While I lull you,
Baby lullaby.

Rock-a-Bye Baby

Rock-a-bye baby on the tree top,
When the wind blows the cradle will rock.
When the bough breaks the cradle will fall,
And down will come baby, cradle and all.

When Little Birdie Bye-Bye Goes

When little Birdie bye-bye goes,
Quiet as mice in churches,
He puts his head where no one knows,
On one leg he perches.

When little Babie bye-bye goes,
On Mother's arm reposing,
Soon he lies beneath the clothes,
Safe in the cradle dozing.

When pretty Pussy goes to sleep,
Tail and nose together,
Then little mice around her creep,
Lightly as a feather.

When little Babie goes to sleep,
And he is very near us,
Then on tip-toe softly creep,
That Babie may not hear us.
Lullaby! Lullaby! Lulla, Lulla, Lullaby!

So, So, Rock-a-By So!

So, so, rock-a-by so!
Off to the garden where dreamikins grow;
And here is a kiss on your winkyblink eyes,
And here is a kiss on your dimpledown cheek
And here is a kiss for the treasure that lies
In the beautiful garden way up in the skies
Which you seek.
Now mind these three kisses wherever you go—
So, so, rock-a-by so!

My Dearest Baby, Go to Sleep

My dearest baby, go to sleep,
For now the bright round moon doth peep
On thy little snow-white bed,
And upon thy pretty head.

The silver stars are shining bright,
And bid my baby dear good-night;
And every bird has gone to rest
Long since in its little nest.

The lambs no longer run and leap,
But by the daisies lie asleep;
The flowers have closed their pretty eyes
Until the sun again shall rise.

Wynken, Blynken, and Nod

Wynken, Blynken, and Nod one night
Sailed off in a wooden shoe—
Sailed on a river of crystal light,
Into a sea of dew.
"Where are you going, and what do you wish?"
The old moon asked the three.
"We have come to fish for the herring fish
That live in this beautiful sea;
Nets of silver and gold have we!"
Said Wynken, Blynken, and Nod.

The old moon laughed and sang a song,
As they rocked in the wooden shoe,
And the wind that sped them all night long
Ruffled the waves of dew.
The little stars were the herring fish
That lived in that beautiful sea—

"Now cast your nets wherever you wish—
Never afeard are we";
So cried the stars to the fishermen three:
Wynken, Blynken, and Nod.

All night long their nets they threw
To the stars in the twinkling foam—
Then down from the skies came the wooden shoe,
Bringing the fishermen home;
'Twas all so pretty a sail it seemed
As if it could not be,
And some folks thought 'twas a dream they'd dreamed
Of sailing that beautiful sea—
But I shall name you the fishermen three:
Wynken, Blynken, and Nod.

Wynken and Blynken are two little eyes,
And Nod is a little head,
And the wooden shoe that sailed the skies
Is a wee one's trundle-bed.
So shut your eyes while mother sings
Of wonderful sights that be,
And you shall see the beautiful things
As you rock in the misty sea,
Where the old shoe rocked the fishermen three:
Wynken, Blynken, and Nod.

Hush-a-Bye Baby

Hush-a-bye baby,
Thy cradle is green,
Father's a nobleman,
Mother's a queen.
Betty's a lady
And wears a gold ring,
John is a drummer
And drums for the king.
Boom-tiddy, boom-tiddy,
Boom, boom, boom.

Lullaby, O Lullaby

Lullaby! O lullaby!
Baby, hush that little cry!
Light is dying,
Bats are flying,
Bees to-day with work have done;
So, till comes the morrow's sun,
Let sleep kiss those bright eyes dry!
Lullaby! O lullaby!

Lullaby! O lullaby!
Hush'd are all things far and nigh;
Flowers are closing,
Birds reposing,
All sweet things with life are done.
Sweet, till dawns the morning sun,
Sleep then kiss those blue eyes dry!
Lullaby! O lullaby!

My Bed Is a Boat

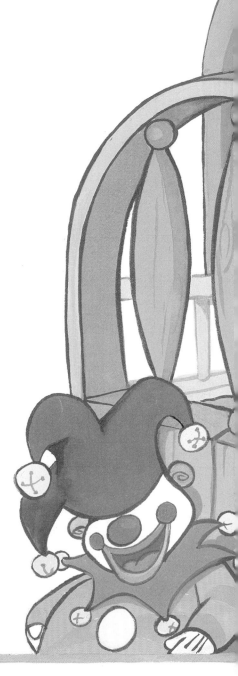

My bed is like a little boat;
Nurse helps me in when I embark;
She girds me in my sailor's coat
And starts me in the dark.

At night, I go on board and say
Good night to all my friends on shore;
I shut my eyes and sail away
And see and hear no more.

And sometimes things to bed I take,
As prudent sailors have to do;
Perhaps a slice of wedding-cake,
Perhaps a toy or two.

All night across the dark we steer;
But when the day returns at last,
Safe in my room, beside the pier,
I find my vessel fast.

Bed in Summer

In winter I get up at night
And dress by yellow candle-light.
In summer, quite the other way,
I have to go to bed by day.

I have to go to bed and see
The birds still hopping on the tree,
Or hear the grown-up people's feet
Still going past me in the street.

And does it not seem hard to you,
When all the sky is clear and blue,
And I should like so much to play,
To have to go to bed by day?

24

25

Sweet and Low

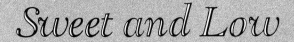

Sweet and low, sweet and low,
Wind of the western sea,
Low, low, breathe and blow,
Wind of the western sea!
Over the rolling waters go,
Come from the dropping moon and
   blow,
Blow him again to me,
While my little one, while my pretty
   one sleeps.

Hush Thee, My Babby

Hush thee, my babby,
Lie still with thy daddy,
Thy mammy has gone to the mill,
To grind thee some wheat
To make thee some meat,
And so, my dear babby, lie still.

Good-Night

Baby, baby, lay your head
On your pretty cradle bed;
Shut your eye-peeps, now the day
And the light are gone away;
All the clothes are tuck'd in tight;
Little baby, dear, good-night.

Yes, my darling, well I know
How the bitter wind doth blow;
And the winter's snow and rain
Patter on the window-pane;
But they cannot come in here,
To my little baby dear.

For the window shutteth fast,
Till the stormy night is past,
And the curtains warm are spread
Roundabout her cradle bed;
So till morning shineth bright,
Little baby, dear, good-night.

Young Night Thought

All night long and every night,
When my mama puts out the light,
I see the people marching by,
As plain as day, before my eye.

Armies and emperors and kings,
All carrying different kinds of things,
And marching in so grand a way,
You never saw the like by day.

So fine a show was never seen
At the great circus on the green;
For every kind of beast and man
Is marching in that caravan.

At first they move a little slow,
But still the faster on they go,
And still beside them close I keep
Until we reach the town of Sleep.

Golden Slumbers

Golden slumbers kiss your eyes,
Smiles awake you when you rise.
Sleep, pretty darling, do not cry,
And I will sing a lullaby,
Lullaby, lullaby, lullaby.

Care you know not, therefore sleep,
While I o'er you watch do keep.
Sleep, pretty darling, do not cry,
And I will sing a lullaby,
Lullaby, lullaby, lullaby.